Getting To Know...

Nature's Children

TURTLES

Merebeth Switzer

PUBLISHER	Joseph R. DeVarennes
PUBLICATION DIRECTOR	Kenneth H. Pearson
MANAGING EDITOR	Valerie Wyatt
SERIES ADVISOR	Merebeth Switzer
SERIES CONSULTANT	Michael Singleton
CONSULTANTS	Ross James
	Kay McKeever
	Dr. Audrey N. Tomera
ADVISORS	Roger Aubin
	Robert Furlonger
	Gaston Lavoie
EDITORIAL SUPERVISOR	Jocelyn Smyth
PRODUCTION MANAGER	Ernest Homewood
PRODUCTION ASSISTANTS	Penelope Moir
	Brock Piper

EDITORS
Katherine Farris   Anne Minguet-Patocka
Sandra Gulland   Sarah Reid
Cristel Kleitsch   Cathy Ripley
Elizabeth MacLeod   Eleanor Tourtel
Pamela Martin   Karin Velcheff

PHOTO EDITORS	Bill Ivy
	Don Markle
DESIGN	Annette Tatchell
CARTOGRAPHER	Jane Davie
PUBLICATION ADMINISTRATION	Kathy Kishimoto
	Monique Lemonnier

ARTISTS
Marianne Collins   Greg Ruhl
Pat Ivy   Mary Theberge

This series is approved and recommended by the Federation of Ontario Naturalists.

Canadian Cataloguing in Publication Data

Switzer, Merebeth.
  Turtles

(Getting to know—nature's children)
Includes index.
ISBN 0-7172-1946-1

1. Turtles—Juvenile literature.
I. Title. II. Series.

QL666.C5S97 1985   j597.92   C85-098740-7

Have you ever wondered . . .

If you could look back in time and see the earth as it appeared 200 million years ago, what would you see? Giant trees, strange plants and dinosaurs. But look, what's that? Why it's a turtle. That's right, there were turtles way back in the days of the dinosaurs. And, amazingly, they have changed very little since that time.

Maybe that is why turtles have fascinated people and why there are so many stories and legends about them. You almost certainly know at least one turtle story: Aesop's fable about the Tortoise that races the Hare—and wins! But did you know that ancient legends from places as far apart as China, North America and India say that the earth is carried on the back of a turtle?

Do turtles deserve the reputation for slowness and dependability that stories and legends give them? And how did they survive so much longer than their ancient friends?

Wood Turtle.

Wise Young Turtles

Imagine a long, wide stretch of empty beach. It is the middle of the night, but the moon and stars are out.

Look over there, where the sand meets the trees. Can you see that place where the sand seems to be moving? Watch carefully now. . . isn't that a little dark spot, just there? It's moving this way, toward the water . . . . And there's another one behind it and another.

What can they be, these tiny crawling shapes coming up out of the sand?

They are turtle hatchlings. But where do they come from, and where are they going? And why are these babies out here alone?

One of the truly amazing things about turtles is that they are born knowing almost everything they need to know to cope with the world on their own. Once their mother has prepared their nest, laid her eggs and covered them carefully, she has done all she needs to do for her babies.

And that is only ONE of the amazing things . . . .

Opposite page:

These newly hatched Painted Turtles will not reach their full size until they are five years old. In the wild they may live up to 20 years.

Reptile Relatives

Turtles are reptiles. This means they are relatives of crocodiles, snakes and lizards. All reptiles have certain features in common. For one thing, although some spend a great deal of time in the water, they must breathe air, just as you do.

What else do reptiles have in common? Well, think carefully: have you ever seen a furry snake or a turtle with eyelashes? No? That is because reptiles do not have hair. Instead they have a thick scaly or leathery covering.

Finally, reptiles have no built-in temperature control. While your body stays at more or less the same temperature no matter how cold or hot the weather, a reptile's does not. Its temperature will go up when it is in the sun and down when it moves into the shade.

As you can imagine, this affects how and where reptiles, including turtles, live.

Opposite page:

Often all you see of the Spiny Softshell Turtle is the tip of its snout sticking above the water!

9

Turtle Territory

Turtles are found almost anywhere that it is warm for at least several months of the year. Although they depend on their surroundings to keep their body at the right temperature, they have ways of surviving winters. But in between they need a good period of summer warmth and sunshine.

In North America this means that turtles can live all through the United States and Mexico but only in the southern part of Canada. Some types, such as the Painted and Snapping Turtles, are found in many regions. Others— the Yellow Blotch Map Turtle, for instance— are found only in one small area.

The Eastern Painted Turtle, though common, is shy and difficult to approach.

What's in a Name?

You have probably heard someone call turtles tortoises. And you may have run into yet another name—terrapin.

Fortunately, this is not really as confusing as it may seem. There are many different kinds of turtles, but they fall into three main categories: sea turtles, tortoises or land turtles, and freshwater turtles, sometimes called terrapins.

Whatever they are are called, they are all turtles.

Who's Who

Sea turtles are found in the Atlantic and Pacific oceans and in the Gulf of Mexico. Their legs are flattened, paddle-like flippers and they spend almost all their time in the water. They only come ashore to lay their eggs. Most sea turtles are very large. Many grow to be over 100 kilograms (220 pounds).

Tortoises are turtles that can live only on land. They are are poor swimmers and usually live near deserts and grasslands. You can recognize them by their stump-like legs and their high, rounded shells.

Although some turtles spend their entire lives on land, most spend part of their time in the water and part on land. The turtles you probably know best are the freshwater turtles you might find near your home or cottage or on special country outings. These turtles spend part of their time in the water of lakes, ponds and streams and part on land. They have many different styles of shells and their feet are usually suited for both walking and swimming. Most of these turtles have claws, and some of those that spend a great deal of time in the water have webbed feet.

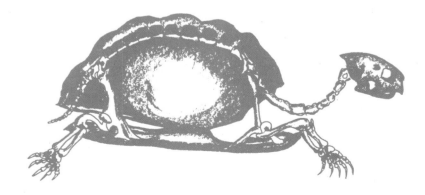

The turtle's shell is part of its body. It is very firmly attached and the turtle could not survive without it.

Built-in Armor

If you were asked to describe a turtle, where would you start? With its shell, of course. After all, to most of us, that is what makes a turtle a turtle.

Turtle shells can look very different, however. They may be high and rounded like that of the tortoise; or low and sleek and streamlined for gliding through water. Or any style in between.

Turtle shells may be brown or green all over or a mottled mixture of dullish shades. Or they may have brightly colored spots, streaks and borders or intricate patterns.

But whatever a turtle's shell looks like, it is bony and hard and it is the turtle's main means of protection. Many turtles can pull their head, tail and legs inside their shell— and they do so at the first hint of danger.

This built-in armor may be one of the reasons that turtles have survived for so many generations.

Opposite page:

The faint yellow lines on its shell give the Map Turtle its name.

A Box Turtle has a large hinged plastron and can withdraw completely into its shell.

Snapping Turtles have very small plastrons and cannot pull their head and legs inside.

Opposite page:

Blanding's Turtle.

Upside/Downside

A turtle's shell is made up of two parts—a top called the carapace and a bottom called the plastron. The parts are usually joined at the sides by bony ridges. At the front and back ends are openings through which the turtle's head, tail and chunky legs stick out.

Both parts of the turtle's shell have an inner layer made up of bony plates that are actually part of the turtle's backbone and ribs. Covering this on most turtles is a layer of broad, thin scales called scutes. These are made of material something like your fingernails.

Sometimes a turtle may have sharp points on its back or other strange looking lumps. These are scutes that are specially built to help it blend into its surroundings or to make it look threatening.

Some turtles shed their scutes as they grow. But new ones are already formed underneath, so this does not leave the turtle without protection.

Stinky Stinkpot

Most grown-up turtles have shells that are strong enough to keep them pretty safe. Babies, however, and some other turtles are so small that their shell does not pose much of a problem for predators.

But some small turtles have another special safety device. The Stinkpot and its close relatives the Mud and Musk Turtles have two glands that produce a strong smelly liquid called musk. When they are disturbed, they release this unpleasant musk all over the intruder. A close encounter with a Stinkpot will show you that its name is well deserved!

The Stinkpot may be small but its smell is mighty.

Clumsy on Land

Turtles are famous for their slowness and it is true that most of them move slowly and awkwardly on land.

Strangely enough, tortoises—the turtles that live entirely on land—move particularly clumsily on their stumpy legs and small feet. No wonder Aesop's Hare thought it had nothing to worry about in its race with the Tortoise!

Freshwater turtles move more quickly on land than most tortoises. Some can even run (though not what you would call *fast*), and some can climb. The Stinkpot, for example, can climb the trunks of small trees to a height of more than two metres (6 feet).

Nonetheless, most freshwater and all sea turtles move most easily in the water. They can swim quite quickly and large sea turtles can cover great distances. They may migrate hundreds of kilometres (miles) to find food or to return to the nesting sites where they hatched to lay their own eggs.

Opposite page:

The Green Sea Turtle has been known to stay underwater for up to five hours.

Lung Power

A turtle breathes through its mouth and nose and uses lungs, just as you do. However, it does have one difficulty.

If you place your hand on your chest you will feel your ribs moving, helping you to breathe. The turtle's ribs, being fixed to its shell, cannot move. But the turtle's body is specially built so that it can make its lungs expand simply by moving its legs.

Many turtles spend a great deal of their time underwater. They still need to breathe. Some have ways for their bodies to take small amounts of oxygen directly from the water. Others have a long, snorkel-like nose that allows them to keep their body underwater while they breathe oxygen from the air. And all of them can slow down their heartbeat when they are underwater, so that their body needs less oxygen. How long they can stay underwater without coming up for air depends on the kind of turtle—and on what it is doing. A swimming turtle uses up oxygen much faster than a resting one.

Opposite page:

Taking a breather. (Blanding's Turtle)

23

Turtle Senses

Turtles do not have the same kind of ears as you. A turtle's ears are flat against its head and are really pieces of skin stretched over the ear opening. People used to think that turtles could not hear sounds but could only feel them through their body. We now know that a turtle can actually hear as well as a cat, and some owners of pet turtles claim that their pet will come when they call.

Turtles see quite well too. Unlike many animals they can see colors and seem to be particularly sensitive to red. And unlike their cousins the snakes, turtles have moveable eyelids and can blink.

Don't worry if you see a turtle gulping air. It is not having trouble breathing. It is simply bringing air into its mouth in order to smell its surroundings and sniff out its next meal.

The Box Turtle can pull itself completely inside its shell and close itself tightly into a nearly enemy-proof box.

Turtle Treats

And speaking of meals, what do turtles like to eat? That depends on the type of turtle and the kinds of food available.

Some types of turtles, especially the tortoises, feed mainly on plants. They are called herbivores. Other types eat only meat. They are called carnivores. The Snapping Turtle is a carnivore. It feeds on insects, crayfish, crabs, snails, fish, frogs, toads, snakes, birds' eggs and small mammals.

Most turtles, however, are omnivores, which means they will eat anything. They do have favorite foods though, and so we are fairly sure they have a keen sense of taste. The Leatherback, for example, has a definite passion for jellyfish, while the Green Sea Turtle eats only eel grass.

Most turtles can go for days or even weeks without eating. But when food is plentiful, they will eat all they can and may become quite fat.

Opposite page:

To avoid the hot sun the Desert Tortoise feeds in the early morning or late afternoon.

Toothless Jaws and Tempting Tongues

To munch all this food you would think that a turtle must have a pretty good set of teeth. This is not the case. In fact, turtles have no teeth at all! They do, however, have a hard beak which has a rough cutting edge that they use to tear apart and sometimes grind their food. Some turtles, such as the Alligator Snapping Turtle, have such a strong beak that they could easily cut a fish in half—and possibly chomp off a finger. With all Snapping Turtles, it is best to let an expert handle them.

A turtle cannot stick out its tongue, but it does have one. It uses its tongue to move food around in its mouth and into its throat. The Alligator Snapping Turtle even has an extra tongue-like growth in its mouth that looks rather like a worm. When the turtle holds its mouth open and wiggles this, it acts like a fishing lure. Soon an unwary fish swims in expecting dinner. Instead, the fish becomes dinner for the turtle.

Opposite page:

A Snapping Turtle cannot hide inside its shell. If attacked it must defend itself, and this may be why it has a reputation for being aggressive. Actually, it will slip away rather than fight if it can.

28

Turtle Talk

Turtles are basically quiet creatures. They live pretty much on their own, and most of them do not have special areas they protect from other turtles. This means that they really have little need to communicate with each other.

Turtles do make sounds, however. Some may grunt and others have a whistling call which they seem to produce mainly at mating time. An angry turtle, especially a young one, will often hiss loudly at an attacker.

When trying to attract or impress a female, some males use silent body language to get their message across. Some wave their long toenails in the face of a female, while others have special ways of bobbing their heads.

Diamondback Terrapin

Passing the Time

Like most animals in the wild, turtles spend a good deal of their waking hours looking for food. Some do this mainly at night, others in the daytime, still others at dawn or dusk.

Because turtles cannot control the temperature of their body, most of them also spend as much time as they can basking in the sun. They must do so to warm themselves up after a long swim or a chilly night.

So if you watch carefully when you are near a pond or marsh on a sunny day, you may see a turtle basking on a log or rock with its neck and legs stretched out and its toes spread wide apart to catch as much of the sun's warmth as possible. In fact, you may see several. Sometimes, if good sunning space is scarce, you might even see one turtle sprawled on top of a larger one's shell.

Always room for one more. (Painted Turtles)

Keeping Cool

Turtles can get *too* hot, however, so they must not wander far from water or from trees or rocks. That way, if a turtle feels too hot while sunbathing, it can simply move into the shade. Or it can dunk itself in the water—just as you might if you were lying on the beach.

But if turtles can get too hot, how do the tortoises of the southwestern United States cope with the high temperatures of the desert?

They cope by digging underground burrows. A burrow is much cooler and more moist than the open desert. Deep in the ground, a tortoise can keep cool and save the precious water its body contains. On very hot days the tortoise will probably not come out of its burrow at all.

Tortoises are the only turtles that build any form of home. All other turtles simply make use of the world around them. A sleepy turtle may snooze at the bottom of a marsh, doze under a log or snuggle down into the mud of a pond.

Opposite page:

Snapping Turtle.

Sleeping away the Winter

Turtles in northern areas would freeze if they could not find a way to avoid winter. So, like some other animals, they hibernate.

As fall approaches and the weather begins to cool, these turtles start to put on extra fat. This will supply what energy they need through the winter. As the temperature drops still more, they gradually get less and less active. Finally they burrow deep into the mud at the bottom of ponds or into the loose soil of the forest floor and settle in to sleep the winter away.

Scientists have found that the blood of hibernating turtles actually changes to work rather like the antifreeze we buy in winter for our cars. As a result, the turtle's body temperature can drop to only a few degrees above freezing—much lower than that of most animals that hibernate.

In the spring, as the soil or water begins to warm, the turtle's body, too, gradually warms up. Finally the turtle awakens, ready to face another year.

Early warm spells in the winter can be dangerous for turtles. If they wake up too soon from their winter sleep, a return to cold weather may catch them unprepared and they may freeze. In fact, winter can be the biggest danger a turtle faces in its adult life.

Nesting Time

Different types of turtles have their young at different ages. Mud Turtles are about five or six years old when they mate, while the Desert Tortoise must wait until it is about 15 years old. Some turtles nest one or more times a year, others may nest only once every few years. A turtle that nests once a year usually lays its eggs in the spring so that they will be kept warm by the heat of the summer sun.

All turtles bury their eggs in sand or soil. Even the sea turtles come ashore and drag themselves a few hundred metres (yards) onto the beach to lay their eggs.

Many turtles have traditional nesting grounds that have been used for generations. The mother's desire to lay her eggs in a certain place is very strong. This can pose a danger as she will try to cross any barrier including backyards, fences and busy highways to reach her nesting ground. Turtles are sometimes hit by cars as they cross roads on their way to lay their eggs.

Opposite page:

A few kinds of turtles do not have scutes. Instead they have a hard leathery skin over their shell that gives them a sleeker, smooth look. (Softshell Turtle)

As Safe as Mom Can Make Them

The mother turtle usually lays her eggs in the middle of the night. This is the safest time for turtles to be out in the open.

First she digs a hole with her hind feet, using her front legs to hold her body in place. After the hole is dug she holds her body over the nest and deposits her eggs in it.

Depending on the type of turtle, the mother may lay one to several hundred eggs. She then covers the nest and packs down the loose soil with her body. She may pack the soil for quite a distance around the nest. This helps to confuse hungry predators.

This female Snapping Turtle may lay as many as 50 eggs in this hole before she is finished.

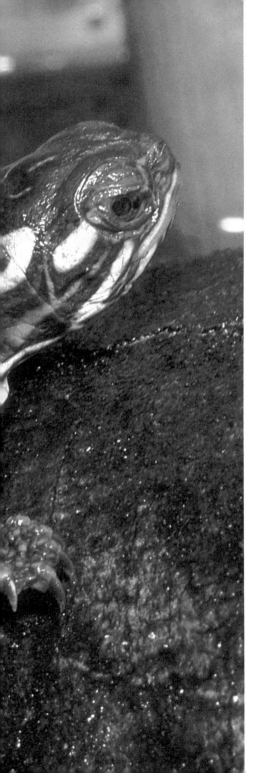

On Their Own

The mother never sees her babies. She leaves her eggs to hatch in the warmth of the sun. It takes two or more months for the eggs to develop. During this time, the leathery roundish eggs may be found and eaten by foxes, skunks, bears, raccoons or other animals. The nest may also be flooded during heavy rains and the eggs washed away, or the eggs may dry out if they are not buried deep enough. But most turtle mothers lay many eggs and this helps insure that some babies will survive.

Young Painted Turtle.

The Long Trek

When a baby turtle is ready to hatch, it must break through the tough shell of the egg. To do this, each hatchling has a special tooth called an egg tooth and uses it to slit the egg open. The tooth falls off within a few days.

Once the baby is out of its shell, it climbs up through the soil or sand to the surface. Some lucky hatchlings emerge to find themselves in or very near a suitable place to live. But many young water turtles must now undertake a long journey. Even if they cannot see the water, they know instinctively in which direction to go. One after another they set out across the stretch of sand or through the woods to find the ocean, marsh or pond their mother came from.

This is another dangerous time in the young turtle's life. Hawks, gulls, raccoons, skunks and even fish see the tiny baby turtles as an easy meal. But the babies seem to know this too, and they will usually surface after dark when there is less danger of being spotted by predators.

Opposite page:

Dangerous journey. (Snapping Turtle)

From Small Beginnings

All turtle hatchlings are tiny, about the size of a quarter. It is hard to believe that some of these helpless little turtles may someday grow up to be giant Leatherback Sea Turtles weighing over 700 kilograms (1500 pounds) and measuring nearly 2.5 metres (8 feet) in length. In fact, some Leatherbacks have weighed more than 1000 kilos (2200 pounds)!

The smaller types of turtles may live up to 5 years, but the larger turtles live much longer. There are many stories that tell of amazingly old turtles, but no one is really sure how long turtles can live. After all, when an animal can live for over 100 years it is hard to keep records!

Big or small, turtles are truly amazing creatures. They have survived remarkable changes in the world around them and with their slow-moving life and their built-in armor they will surely be around for generations to come.

Special Words

Carapace A turtle's top shell.

Carnivore An animal that eats mainly meat.

Herbivore An animal that eats mainly plants.

Hibernate To go into a deep sleep for the entire winter.

Mate To come together to produce young.

Musk A strong smelling substance produced by some animals.

Omnivore An animal that eats both plants and animals.

Plastron A turtle's bottom shell.

Scutes Scaly plates that cover a turtle's shell.

Terrapins Usually used to describe freshwater turtles.

Tortoise Turtles that live only on land. (In some countries, however, *tortoise* is commonly used for freshwater turtles as well.)

INDEX

Cover Photo: Bill Ivy

Photo Credits: Robert C. Simpson (Valan Photos), pages 4, 18, 33; Wayne Lankinen (Valan Photos), page 7; J.D. Markou (Valan Photos), pages 8, 45; Bill Ivy, pages 11, 17, 22, 28, 34, 41; James Richards (Miller Services), page 14; Harold Lambert (Miller Services), page 21; Arthur Holbrook (Miller Services), page 25; Wayne Lynch (Master File), page 26; J.D. Taylor (Miller Services), page 30; Brian Morin (Network Stock Photo File), page 38; Robert McCaw (Network Stock Photo File), page 42.

Getting To Know...

Nature's Children

BEES

Elin Kelsey

PUBLISHER	Joseph R. DeVarennes		
PUBLICATION DIRECTOR	Kenneth H. Pearson		
MANAGING EDITOR	Valerie Wyatt		
SERIES ADVISOR	Merebeth Switzer		
SERIES CONSULTANT	Michael Singleton		
CONSULTANTS	Ross James		
	Kay McKeever		
	Dr. Audrey N. Tomera		
ADVISORS	Roger Aubin		
	Robert Furlonger		
	Gaston Lavoie		
EDITORIAL SUPERVISOR	Jocelyn Smyth		
PRODUCTION MANAGER	Ernest Homewood		
PRODUCTION ASSISTANTS	Penelope Moir		
	Brock Piper		
EDITORS	Katherine Farris	Anne Minguet-Patocka	
	Sandra Gulland	Sarah Reid	
	Cristel Kleitsch	Cathy Ripley	
	Elizabeth MacLeod	Eleanor Tourtel	
	Pamela Martin	Karin Velcheff	
PHOTO EDITORS	Bill Ivy		
	Don Markle		
DESIGN	Annette Tatchell		
CARTOGRAPHER	Jane Davie		
PUBLICATION ADMINISTRATION	Kathy Kishimoto		
	Monique Lemonnier		
ARTISTS	Marianne Collins	Greg Ruhl	
	Pat Ivy	Mary Theberge	

This series is approved and recommended
by the Federation of Ontario Naturalists.

Canadian Cataloguing in Publication Data

Kelsey, Elin.
    Bees

(Getting to know—nature's children)
Includes index.
ISBN 0-7172-1900-3

1. Bees —Juvenile literature.
I. Title. II. Series.

QL568.A6K44 1985   j595.799   C85-098702-4

Have you ever wondered . . .

Bzzzz! A busy honeybee buzzes by you on its way through your garden. Did you know that without the labors of honeybees like this one there would not be any honey to spread on your toast in the morning?

The bees you may see in your garden are worker bees. They live in a hive which is a bit like a castle. Deep inside this castle lives its ruler, the queen bee. She is fed and guarded by thousands of female worker bees. Also living in the castle are the male bees, or drones.

There are more than 22 000 kinds of bees in the world, but only honeybees live in hives and produce large amounts of honey. Let's take a closer look at the hard-working honeybee and at life inside the hive.

Honeybees were not found in North America until the seventeenth century when settlers brought them.

Bumble bee

Honeybee

Bee Basics

Everyone knows what a honeybee looks like. Its thick, round body and yellow and black stripes make it easy to spot. Insect-eating animals quickly learn that those stripes can mean a painful sting. In fact, the bee's stripes are such a good "stay away" warning that a few non-stinging insects have copied the striped pattern. These copycats are mistaken for bees and left alone.

Like all insects, a bee has six legs and its body is made up of three parts. It has a round head, a middle section called a thorax and an egg-shaped section on the end called an abdomen. Bees do not have bones. Instead, they have a hard outer "skin," called an exoskeleton, that supports their bodies from the outside.

This Beefly looks dangerous thanks to its resemblance to the honeybee, but it couldn't sting even if it wanted to.

Sensitive Bee Senses

You find out about the world through your eyes, ears, nose and fingers. A honeybee gets its information about what is happening in the world through its eyes, feelers and body hairs.

The bee has two enormous eyes which cover the whole sides of its head. Each eye is divided into more than 4000 tiny parts. When you see a flower, you see a single picture. But a bee probably sees a flower made up of thousands of little squares. Look through a fine wire screen at something and you will get an idea of how a bee might see.

Bees cannot see the color red—to them it looks like black. However they can see other colors that you cannot, just as dogs can hear sounds that you cannot.

In addition to its two large eyes the honeybee has three smaller eyes on the top of its head. If you look carefully you can see one of them on this bee.

A bee does not use a nose to smell as you do. Instead it smells with a pair of long furry feelers called antennae. But these antennae do more than just smell. By sticking them into a jar of jam, a bee not only knows how the jam smells, but how it tastes and feels too.

Bees also sense things through their hair. Each hair on the bee's fuzzy coat is as sensitive as a cat's whisker. These sensitive hairs help the honeybee to sense what is going on around it, particularly things that it cannot see. If a strange air current tickles the body hairs, the bee buzzes off.

The honeybee's sensitive antennae are constantly at work smelling and tasting everything they contact.

Weather Sense

If you are planning a picnic, keep an eye out for bees. Lots of bees around means the weather will probably be fine for a picnic. If the bees have disappeared, think twice. You might be in for rain. But how do the bees know that? They know because they can detect changes in the air pressure. A sudden drop in air pressure tells the bees that rain is on the way, and they do not leave the hive.

Rain is not the only thing that keeps bees in their hive. If the temperature falls below 10 degrees Celsius (50 degrees Fahrenheit), you will never see any bees. It is simply too cold for them to fly.

Cold-weather Clusters

Like all insects, bees cannot completely control their body temperature. When they are outside the temperature of their bodies is about as warm—or as cold—as the air around them. And the colder it gets, the more slowly they move. When it gets really cold they can barely move at all, let alone fly.

On cold days the bees huddle inside their hive. The ones on the cold outer edges of the hive try to force their way farther in to keep warm. Even when it is below freezing outside, bees can make their hive as warm as a summer afternoon by clustering in this way.

Flying Aces

Sometimes in the summer the hive gets too hot instead of too cold. Then the bees use their built-in air conditioners to cool down their home. They simply flap their wings!

Every bee has two sets of wings—a large strong pair in the front and a small round pair hooked to the front ones. The wings on the right side of a bee always work together as do those on the left. Each wing is as thin and clear as a piece of plastic wrap. They may look too frail to lift a bee into the air, but do not be fooled. A honeybee can perform a most impressive air show.

For instance, if a worker bee suddenly spots a tasty flower, it can turn in mid-air and dive in for a closer look. After hovering for a moment, it might zoom off and then up, perhaps as high as your bedroom ceiling before flying on. Most amazing of all, in the time it takes you to blink, a flying bee flaps its wings 250 times.

Opposite page:

A worker honeybee's powerful wings will carry her five kilometres (3 miles) in just 12 minutes.

17

Honeycomb Hives

Many bees are kept by beekeepers and "farmed" for their honey. The beekeeper provides sturdy wooden boxes for the bees to build their hive in. But wild honeybees must make their own homes. They build hives in the hole of a hollow tree or in a rock crevice by glueing together thousands upon thousands of tiny wax rooms called cells.

Believe it or not, all the wax used for building comes from the bees themselves. It is made in special glands under their abdomens. With their feet, they scoop tiny flakes of the wax into their mouths. Then, just as you would tackle a hard piece of bubble gum, the bees soften the wax by chewing it. When the wax is soft the bees make the six-sided wax cells.

Most of these cells will be used for raising young worker bees and storing food. Slightly larger cells are built for the drones. And long thin cells are built for the queen bees.

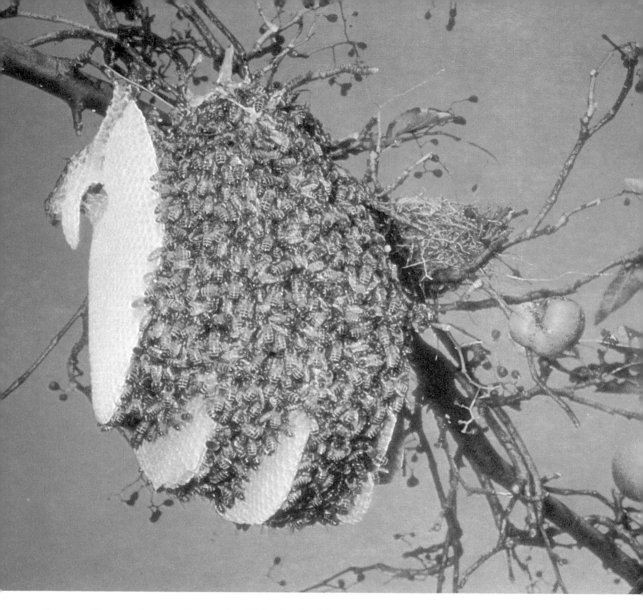

Sometimes honeybees build their hives in the open hanging from tree branches.

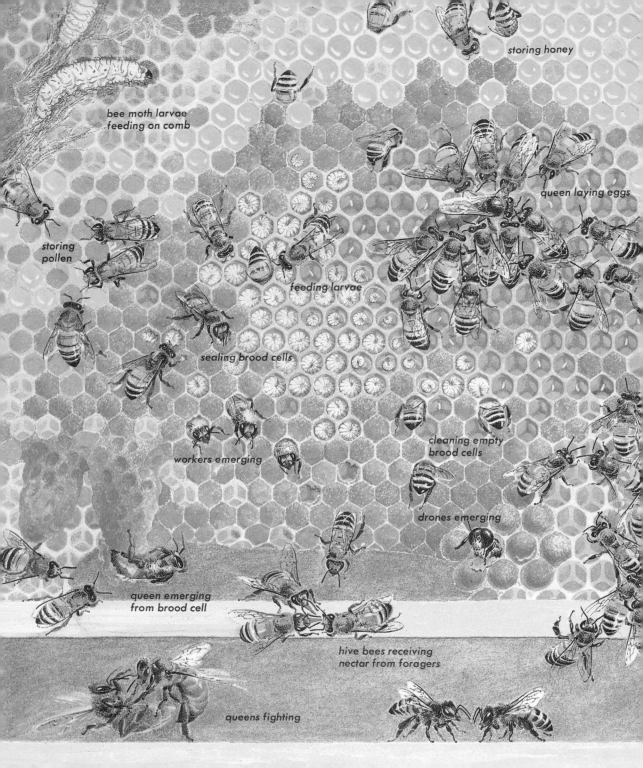

storing honey

bee moth larvae
feeding on comb

queen laying eggs

storing
pollen

feeding larvae

sealing brood cells

cleaning empty
brood cells

workers emerging

drones emerging

queen emerging
from brood cell

hive bees receiving
nectar from foragers

queens fighting

ACTIVITIES INSIDE
A HONEYBEE HIVE

capping honey cells

scout performing
honey dance

building new
comb cells

ejecting drones

fanning and guarding
the hive entrance

Jobs for Everyone

Size comparison

Queen

Worker

Drone

All the hive-building work is done by the worker bees. And so is the housecleaning and food gathering. What then do the drones and the queen bee do?

The drone's job is to mate with the queen, and her job is to lay eggs so that there will always be new bees hatching. So, as you can see, each of the three types of honeybees has a special role in insuring the survival of the hive.

Both the queen and the drone are larger than the worker. The queen is the longest member of her colony. She is also the skinniest. The drone is fatter than the worker and the queen, and he has enormous eyes that cover most of the top of his head.

The queen and drone bees rarely leave the hive. When they do, they fly far higher than the worker bees, so we rarely see them.

The queen bee has been marked with a white spot. She will live about two or three years.

22

Moving Houses

A new hive is started when an older hive gets too large. Somehow the queen bee instinctively knows it is time for her to find new quarters. But before she leaves the old hive, she lays eggs in the long thin cells. These eggs are called royal eggs because they will grow into queen bees. These queen eggs are fed a special baby food called royal jelly.

When the new queens begin to hatch, the old queen can leave. She sends out scouts to find a new place for a hive. As soon as a good place is found, the old queen flies to it, followed by thousands of workers. This flying mass of bees is called a swarm. Bees usually swarm and build new hives in the spring.

A large swarm of honeybees may contain as many as 10 000 individuals!

Queenly Duties

At the old hive, one new queen gets rid of all the others: there is only room for one queen in each hive. Then the new queen flies out, chased by the drones. The drones that catch and mate with her become the fathers of all the eggs that will be laid in the queen's lifetime.

A drone's life is easy, but it is also short. Soon after the queen has mated, the drones are turned away from the hive. Without the workers to feed them, the drones quickly die. However, the queen is treated royally when she returns to the hive. The workers pamper her and protect her as she begins to lay her eggs.

Amazing as it may seem, a queen can lay up to 1500 eggs in a single day. Over her lifetime, she may lay over one million eggs! She lays each of them in a special nursery cell and then has nothing more to do with them.

Royal cell-building.

Baby Boomers

Bee eggs are so tiny that one of them could fit on the dot of this "i." After just three days, a little white grub hatches out of each egg. These wormlike creatures do not look like adult bees—they do not have wings or legs or even proper heads.

The grubs are fed immediately by worker bees. They eat so much that they grow to adult size in just six days. Royal jelly is the secret to the grubs' amazing growth. Queen grubs eat royal jelly for six straight days. Worker and drone grubs are only fed it for three days. For the next three days, they eat a watery mixture of honey and pollen.

Looking after these white grubs is no easy task for the worker bees since each one has to be fed 1300 times a day.

A Rest Before Hatching

After their six-day feast, the grubs are sealed back into their nursery cells. Inside these cozy rooms they spin themselves cocoons and begin to change into adult bees.

The workers make sure the temperature of the hive is just right for the grubs. If the hive cools down, thousands of workers huddle together to warm it up. If it gets too warm, the workers sprinkle water on the cells and fan them with their wings.

In less than two weeks, the grubs become adult bees. They tear open their nursery cells and pop out, fully grown.

A worker's work is never done!

Bee of All Trades

Most of the hatching honeybees are females. They will become the worker bees of the hive and have many jobs—janitor, nurse, construction worker, security guard and food finder.

For the first three weeks, the new worker bees help out inside the hive. They clean cells, feed grubs, make wax for building and repairing the honeycombs or become guards at the hive entrances.

After about three weeks the young bees may leave the hive and search for food. They start by making short flights close to the hive until they learn how to find their way home from faraway fields.

Being a worker bee is such hard work that most of them look scruffy by the time they are four weeks old. Although the workers that are born in the fall usually live through the winter, spring and summer workers rarely live more than six weeks.

Opposite page:

The dandelion is a favorite honeybee feeding station.

Good to the Last Drop

How often have you poked your nose into a flower only to find yourself face to face with a bee? You only stopped for a sniff, but the bee was there for a tasty meal! Everything a bee needs to eat can be found inside a flower.

Try plucking a clover blossom and nibbling the base of its petals. What do you taste? Something very sweet? This sugary juice is called nectar. In some flowers the nectar is hard to reach. But the bee is well prepared for this. It has a built-in drinking straw called a proboscis. Just as you use a straw to slurp up those last delicious drops, a bee uses its proboscis to suck up the tiny nectar droplets.

A honeybee worker carries most of the nectar back to the hive in its stomach. Instead of having just one stomach like we do, a bee has two. It uses one stomach to digest some of the nectar for food. The rest goes into a special honey stomach to be taken back to the hive.

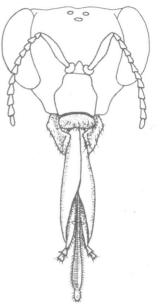

Honeybee proboscis

Opposite page:

In winter, when there are no flowers in the fields to provide nectar, honeybees live on honey, nature's liquid gold.

Honey Factory

As the workers are flying in the field they begin to turn the nectar they have gathered into honey. The nectar is pumped in and out of their honey stomach to remove some of the water in it. When they reach the hive, the field bees squirt this sweet liquid into a cell. Other bees work on the nectar to remove even more water. Finally, when the honey is ready, it is sealed in a wax storage cell.

Making honey is no easy task. Even though a bee's honey stomach is little bigger than a grain of rice, it may take as many as 1000 flower visits to fill it. To make just one thimbleful of honey, a single bee probably works ten hours a day for six days straight. That is hard work!

Hard at work making honey.

Pollen Baskets

The honeybee is one of nature's gardeners. Many flowers cannot use their own pollen to make seeds. They must get it from other flowers. But how, since they cannot move around?

Each time a bee visits a flower, some of the flower's powdery pollen gets caught in the hair on its body and legs. The bee spreads this pollen from flower to flower. Bees' work of spreading pollen is so important that some farmers put hives in orchards, fields and gardens so the bees and flowers are close together.

Pollen is also part of the bees' baby food. Using a built-in comb and brush on its legs, the bee collects the pollen from her hair and mouth parts. She carries it home to the hive in pollen baskets on her hind legs.

Her pollen baskets full, this honeybee will soon head for home.

Dance Directions

When you make an exciting discovery you use words to tell your friends about it. When a bee finds a new patch of sweet flowers it passes on the message to other bees in the hive by *dancing*. Honeybees have two dances—a round dance and a waggle. The bee does a round dance if the flowers are nearby and waggles for places farther away.

As the bee begins to dance, the other bees cluster around her to study her movements, smell the hairs on her body and taste the nectar she has collected. From these clues they will know what kind of flower to look for and where.

First those closest to the dancer join in the frenzied dance. Soon a long train of bees dances behind the leader to pass the message on. The new bees do not need to follow the dancer to the new flower patch. After they have been given the dance directions, they can make a beeline for the flowers all by themselves.

Silent Scent Signals

Bees have another way of communicating besides dancing. They send scent messages for other bees to smell. They use special scents to mark their hives and warn trespassers to stay out. The queen produces another scent to tell the drones when she is ready to mate. And if you have ever been stung by a bee, you were probably marked by a bee's scent message too. It warned other bees to be careful—YOU were dangerous!

The honeybee uses its stinger as a weapon to defend its colony.

Ouch!

Being stung by a bee will hurt you, and it will probably kill the bee. The bee's tiny stinger gets hooked so firmly in your skin that the bee tears its body when it tries to fly away. The bee will die after losing its stinger.

When it stings the bee leaves a tiny drop of venom under your skin. It is the venom that causes the puffy itchy red spot on your skin.

Some people think that bees sting because they are naturally bad tempered but this is not true. A bee will only sting if it is caught or hurt or if it feels that that the hive is in danger. The main danger comes from other animals that want to get at the sweet treat inside the hive.

Bears, skunks and even "robber" bees from other colonies will brave a stinging for a tasty honey lunch. To warn of an attack, the hive has guard bees. They stand at the hive entrances, and use their antennae to pick up any strange vibrations or odors. If the guards sense danger, they quickly pass the message through the hive and the counterattack begins.

Worker bee's stinger

Venom duct

Barbs

Opposite page:

Anytime you see a bee on a flower you can be sure it is a female since only the females work.

45

Honeybees Forever!

Honeybees will fight to protect their queen and their hive. They will even die to make sure their hive is safe.

Every honeybee in the hive has its own job to do. The queen lays her eggs so that there will always be bees to take care of the hive. In another part of the castlelike hive the drones wait for food and the next queen's mating flight. And the tireless little worker bees buzz endlessly in and out and around the hive. Out to the flowers they fly and back again to store the thick sweet food that has made them famous—honey. Mmm, mmm—long live the honeybee colonies of the world!

Special Words

Antennae A pair of sensitive feelers on the top of the bee's head.

Cocoon The silky covering that a bee grub spins around itself while it is changing into an adult.

Cells Tiny six-sided wax rooms where young bees develop and honey and wax are stored.

Colony A group of bees that live together in a hive.

Drone A male bee.

Exoskeleton The hard outer covering which forms a bee's body.

Grub A baby bee.

Hive A bee's home.

Honeycomb Rows of wax cells in which honey is stored and the eggs are laid.

Honey stomach One of a bee's two stomachs which is used for carrying nectar.

Nectar A sweet juice that is made by flowers.

Pollen A sticky powder that all flowers make and many exchange to make seeds.

Proboscis A hollow tube like a drinking straw attached to a bee's mouth and used to suck up nectar.

Queen The leader of a bee colony and the one who lays the eggs.

Royal jelly A special baby food that the worker bees make and feed to the grubs.

Swarm A large number of worker bees with a queen that have left their hive to start a new colony.

Venom A poison that a bee leaves behind after stinging.

Workers The female bees who build and guard the hive, look after the queen and gather food.

INDEX

Cover Photo: Robert C. Simpson (Valan Photos).
Photo Credits: Bill Ivy, pages 4, 8, 11, 12, 15, 16, 23, 28, 33, 34, 38, 40, 43, 44;
V. Claerhout, page 7; Treat Davidson (Miller Services), pages 19, 37; Harold
Lambert (Miller Services), page 24; Michel Bourque (Valan Photos), pages 27,
31. Illustration, pages 20-21 by Arabelle Wheatley, courtesy of *Encyclopedia
Americana*.

Printed and Bound in Spain